D1738982

CELTIC KISSES

To_____

From_____

With Love and Kisses

Celtic Kisses

De-ann Black

WOLFHOUND PRESS
Celebrating 25 Years

Published in 2000 by
Wolfhound Press Ltd
68 Mountjoy Square
Dublin 1, Ireland

The Arts Council
An Chomhairle Ealaíon

Wolfhound Press receives financial assistance from the Arts Council/ An Chomhairle Ealaíon, Dublin.

British Library Cataloguing in Publication Data
A catalogue record for this book is available from the British Library.

ISBN 0-86327-792-6

10 9 8 7 6 5 4 3 2 1

Cover illustration: Aileen Caffrey
Cover design: Mark O'Neill
Typesetting: Wolfhound Press
Printed by Edelvives, Spain

Contents

The Key to Paradise

reek poets described the kiss as the 'key to paradise', able to unlock the heart's deepest desires. Paradise lay beyond the lips of a lover and was an unspoken promise of adoration.

The romance and history of the kiss dates back to our earliest Celtic ancestors, who believed it had magic powers. The breath of a kiss was thought to contain the essence of life and when lovers caressed it was a true mingling of the souls.

Throughout history, the kiss has been a timeless act of love and devotion. It is said that one heartfelt kiss is equal to a thousand words. Few gestures convey our feelings as magically as a kiss, casting an enchanting spell over two lovers.

The Art of Kissing

Kissing is a treasured legacy gifted to us by our ancestors and it is an intriguing reflection of our original nature. Lovers have evolved since primitive times but the sensation of a kiss remains unchanged.

To caress with the lips expresses a host of emotions, from tenderness to passion, depending on the intensity of the act. This touching gesture is fabled to be the heart and soul of our existence, essentially the pure breath of life.

The art of kissing requires two special things — a moment of romance and the strength of desire between two lovers.

Sweet Caress

hy do we venture to 'blow a kiss' to someone we adore? Why do we attempt to steal one? The reasons can be found within the realms of Celtic courtship.

When we blow a kiss it is a secret gesture of forbidden love. Hundreds of years ago, society considered public displays of romantic affection to be vulgar. A young woman was forbidden to kiss a suitor and likewise he was banned from kissing her. This led to secret kisses being blown to each other from a distance.

Stealing a kiss owes its origins to the roguish behaviour of free-spirited young men who literally stole a kiss from any woman who caught their fancy. Usually it was stolen in a playful and light-hearted way.

Sealed with a Kiss

hen sending personal letters to loved ones, we often write the letter X beside the signature to denote a kiss. This dates back to the Middle Ages, when a cross was used to sign important documents. Many people were illiterate, so the cross was adopted as a sworn oath of truth. Eventually this became a symbol of truth and love.

Two kisses entwined were also used as a 'seal' on the flap of an envelope to ensure that the contents remained private until opened by the person for whom they were intended. If the kisses were broken, the note had been tampered with.

Saint Valentine's Day is the most popular day of the year for lovers to exchange written messages of adoration — sealed with a kiss.

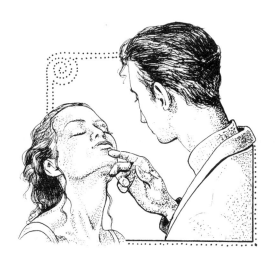

X Appeal

ouch is often referred to as 'the mother of senses', and our lips are surely our most sensitive touch-zone. Even the slightest touch ignites our deepest emotions, revealing the potent power of kissing. By nature we are drawn to kiss each other, to feel the wonderful sensations caressing stirs within us.

Kissing appeals to our basic instincts and is a universal pleasure. In our hearts we yearn for love and deep affection. According to Celtic lore:

> Hearts ablaze with passion
> Will light the darkest night above;
> Hearts afire with true desire
> Will win the greatest love.

Celtic Kisses

Irish and Scottish kissing customs have their origins in the mists of time — in the days when tales of myth and magic were part of everyday life. In the Scottish Highlands there was allegedly a mythical 'loch of dreams' in a hidden valley where lovers met and exchanged courtship vows and kisses. This led to the custom of always kissing a loved one if you caught sight of your joint reflection when near a loch, river or sea.

Irish kissing customs tend to have a little bit of magic involved. For instance, it was customary for lovers to kiss beneath a starlit sky and wish for a happy life together. If either of them saw a shooting star or any other magical sign in the sky, it was a sign that their wish had been granted.

A Moment of Romance

Celtic art depicts unforgettable moments of romance. These timeless embraces capture the heart of romance, creating within us the feeling of a lover's kiss to linger in the memory.

Kiss and Tell

To kiss the bride on her wedding day brings good luck. The groom should be the first to kiss his new bride to seal their marriage vows. One particular Celtic wedding custom was for the bride to wear a circle of flowers as a head-dress, to ensure that the union blossomed and that the couple would be encircled with love forever.

'Kiss-me' is the secret name given to the wild pansy. According to folklore, the flower protected lovers' secret trysts in exchange for a kiss. It was favoured by the fairies and was supposed to have magical powers.

Under the Mistletoe

Kissing under the mistletoe began centuries ago, when it was customary to embrace at Christmastime under a Holy Bough made of evergreens. The bough comprised mistletoe and holly entwined into a decorative loop. Later, this seasonal display became known as the Holly Bough, then finally the Kissing Bough, which was made mainly of mistletoe. Today, only a sprig of mistletoe is used, but this kissing custom is as popular as ever.

Kissing Games

The oldest known kissing game is called Kiss-in-the-ring. It originated hundreds of years ago and was considered to be quite an amorous pastime. The rules of the game were simple. A group of friends formed a wide circle; then one of the players chased another round the ring. If a player was caught, the forfeit was a kiss.

The 'kissing dance' was created in olden days when Celtic reels were popular. During the dance, couples joined hands and skip-stepped to lively music. The dancers would then form an arch by raising their hands, and everyone kissed in turn as they danced under the arch.

Lip Lore

ipstick dates back four thousand years. Deep red dye obtained from berries was used to stain the lips.

Ancient Celtic warriors painted their lips with the dye, believing that each breath they took contained the essence of life, and that the rich red dye would protect the mouth from harm. The ferocious colour was also thought to cast fear into the hearts of the enemy.

While men were the first to wear lipstick, women later claimed it for themselves to use as a beautifying cosmetic.

Traditionally, the colour of a woman's lips is linked to precious gems, which in turn reflect her true character. Lips of rose-pink crystal belong to those with soft, sweet natures; lips of ruby red indicate fire and passion; while peach-coloured coral lips denote a sensual disposition.

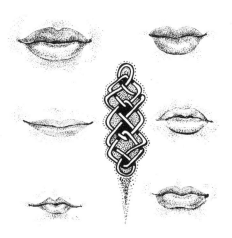

What Your Lips Reveal

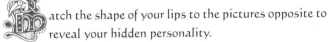 atch the shape of your lips to the pictures opposite to reveal your hidden personality.

- ✖ Generous lips indicate a fun-loving, broad-minded and extroverted character.

- ✖ Curvaceous lips express a good sense of humour and a passionate nature.

- ✖ Slender-shaped lips belong to those with secretly sensual personalities.

- ✖ Pouting lips give the impression of raw sensuality, but may hide a sensitive soul.

- ✖ Rosebud lips reveal a sweet, affectionate, but somewhat reserved nature.

- ✖ An expressive lower lip shows a deeply loving heart, and often belongs to a creative dreamer.

29

A Kiss Farewell

lthough we kiss farewell today
        I know within my heart
Our love will stand the test of time
        When we are far apart.